Elephants

By Anna Prokos

Children's Press®

An Imprint of Scholastic Inc.

Content Consultant
Adam Felts
Curator, Asia Quest and Heart of Africa
Columbus Zoo and Aquarium

Library of Congress Cataloging-in-Publication Data
Names: Prokos, Anna, author.
Title: Elephants/by Anna Prokos.
Other titles: Nature's children (New York, N.Y.)
Description: New York, NY: Children's Press, an imprint of Scholastic Inc., 2018. |
Series: Nature's children | Includes index.
Identifiers: LCCN 2017035458| ISBN 9780531234792 (library binding) | ISBN 9780531245095 (pbk.)
Subjects: LCSH: Elephants—Juvenile literature. | Elephants—Behavior—Juvenile literature.
Classification: LCC QL737.P98 P76 2018 | DDC 599.67—dc23
LC record available at https://lccn.loc.gov/2017035458

Design by Anna Tunick Tabachnik

Creative Direction: Judith Christ-Lafond for Scholastic

Produced by Spooky Cheetah Press

Printed in North Mankato, MN, USA   113

SCHOLASTIC, CHILDREN'S PRESS, NATURE'S CHILDREN™, and associated logos
are trademarks and/or registered trademarks of Scholastic Inc.

1 2 3 4 5 6 7 8 9 10 R 27 26 25 24 23 22 21 20 19 18

Scholastic Inc., 557 Broadway, New York, NY 10012.

Photos ©: cover: Svetlana Foote/Shutterstock; 1: sevenke/Shutterstock; 4 leaf silo and throughout: stockgraphicdesigns.com;
5 elephant silos and throughout: Arttii Univerz/Shutterstock; 5 child silo: All-Silhouettes.com; 5 bottom: Cesare Naldi/Getty
Images; 7: bugphai/iStockphoto; 8 top: goodze/iStockphoto; 8 bottom: Martyn Colbeck/Getty Images; 11: Jaroslaw Grudzinski/
Shutterstock; 12-13: Christophe Boisvieux/Getty Images; 14-15: Nigel Pavitt/Getty Images; 17: Jeryco/iStockphoto; 18-19: John
Lund/Getty Images; 20-21: fotoslav/Shutterstock; 22-23: Karine Aigner/Getty Images; 25: Richard Du Toit/Minden Pictures;
26-27: Konrad Wothe/Minden Pictures; 28-29: Martyn Colbeck/Getty Images; 30-31: Barbara Von Hoffmann/Animals
Animals/Earth Scenes/National Geographic Creative; 33: Warren Photographic/Getty Images; 34-35: Santhosh Varghese/
Shutterstock; 37: Frans Lanting Studio/Alamy Images; 38-39: pamelaoliveras/Getty Images; 40-41: CARL DE SOUZA/AFP/
Getty Images; 42 left: Wildlife Bildagentur GmbH/KimballStock; 42 center left: Joel Sartore/Getty Images; 42 center right:
Farinoza/Dreamstime; 42 right: Jen Guyton/NPL/Minden Pictures; 43 bottom: PytyCzech/iStockphoto; 43 top center: James
R.D. Scott/Getty Images; 43 top right: Africa Media Online/Alamy Images; 43 top left: sevenke/Shutterstock.

Maps by Jim McMahon.

Table of Contents

Fact File: Elephants

World Distribution
Africa and Southeast Asia

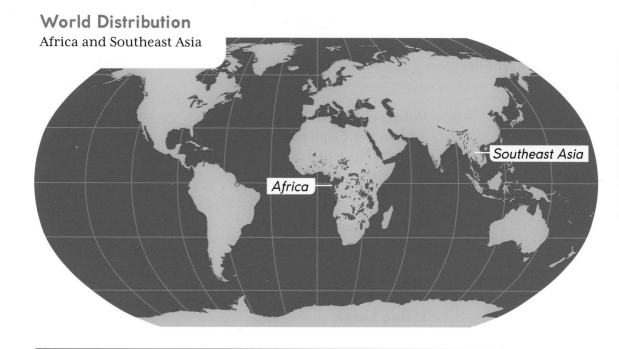

Southeast Asia

Africa

Population Status
African elephants are vulnerable; Asian elephants are endangered

Habitats
Savannas, grassy plains, and woodlands in Africa; tropical forests in Asia

Habits
Females live in groups with their young; communicate with rumbles, grunts, and loud trumpeting

Diet
Mainly leaves and branches of bushes and trees; also vegetation, grasses, and fruit

Distinctive Features
Massive body with wrinkled skin; long, muscular trunk that can grip; huge, floppy ears

Fast Fact
An elephant's skin is 10 percent of its total body weight.

Average Height

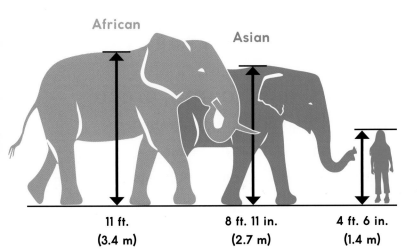

African

Asian

| 11 ft. | 8 ft. 11 in. | 4 ft. 6 in. |
| (3.4 m) | (2.7 m) | (1.4 m) |

Elephants (at shoulder)

Human (age 10)

Taxonomy

CLASS
Mammalia
(mammals)

ORDER
Proboscidea
(elephants)

FAMILY
Elephantidae
(elephants)

GENUS
Loxodonta
(African)
Elephas
(Asian)

SPECIES
• *africana*
  (African)
• *maximus*
  (Asian)

◄ Asian elephants are trained from when they are very young. Their trainers are called mahouts.

CHAPTER 1

Vulnerable Giants

It's a hot afternoon in the damp, green forest. Giant leaves and soft mud keep creatures shaded and cool. Bird songs and cricket chirps fill the air. Suddenly the ground trembles. A loud trumpet blasts. A wall of forty thick legs shifts over the ground. A herd of elephants is on the move.

Elephants are the world's largest land animals. Before they encountered humans, these majestic **mammals** had little to fear in the wild. Sadly, times have changed.

Asian elephants used to live in nearly every forest of Earth's largest continent. Over the years, they have lost 85 percent of their range to humans.

African elephants have lost their **habitat**, too. And they face another problem: **poachers** who kill them for their tusks. These threats have put both elephant **species** in danger. If we are not careful, they could become **extinct**.

▶ Fatty, padded toes and spongy feet help this massive beast stroll along silently.

Asian Elephant

African Elephant

Meet the Elephants

There are two different species of elephants. The first, the African elephant, is the larger and taller of the two. African savanna elephants live in the grasslands of Africa. African forest elephants make their home in Africa's tropical forests, mainly near the Congo River.

The second, the Asian elephant, is slightly smaller than its African cousin. Asian elephants are forest dwellers. The three subspecies of Asian elephants are Sumatran, Borneo, and Sri Lankan.

You can easily tell the difference between the two elephant species by looking at their heads. African elephants have a single large dome. Asian elephants have two humps on top of their heads. The ears of an African elephant are large and shaped like the continent of Africa. Asian elephants have smaller, more rounded ears.

Asian and African elephants have different diets, too. Asian elephants prefer palms, bamboo, and grasses. African elephants eat shrubs and trees.

◀ Asian and African elephants have a lot in common, too! They both have wrinkly gray skin and long trunks.

From Nose to Tail

There is no mistaking an elephant for any other
animal. Its massive size sets this gentle giant apart
from all others. Long trunks are also unique to
elephants, which are part of the Proboscidea order.
As if that weren't enough, the elephant possesses a
number of other unique features, too.

The elephant has very thick skin that is
also very wrinkly. It's made up of thousands
of folds. Scientists think the folds keep the
animals cool by trapping moisture close to their bodies.

Both male and female African elephants grow tusks.
But only some Asian elephants can grow these modified
incisor teeth. Elephants use their tusks to strip bark from
trees, to dig for water, and to protect themselves. Just as
people are right- or left-handed, elephants favor one tusk
over the other. The favored tusk is usually shorter from
wear and tear.

Fast Fact
Young elephants
may hold on to an
elder's tail as
they walk.

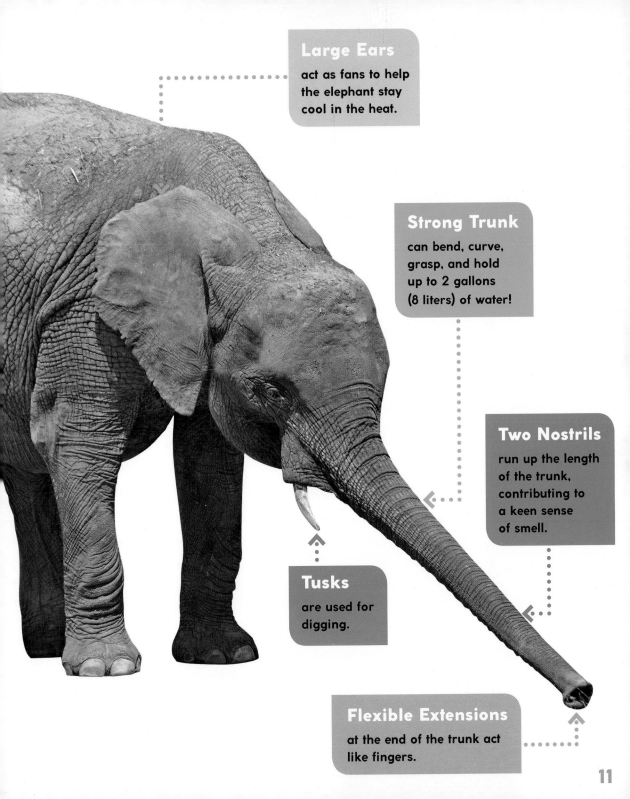

Large Ears
act as fans to help the elephant stay cool in the heat.

Strong Trunk
can bend, curve, grasp, and hold up to 2 gallons (8 liters) of water!

Two Nostrils
run up the length of the trunk, contributing to a keen sense of smell.

Tusks
are used for digging.

Flexible Extensions
at the end of the trunk act like fingers.

11

No Bones About It

The most amazing part of an elephant's body is its trunk. This long organ extends from an elephant's lip down to its toes. But if you looked at an elephant's skeleton, you would never know it had a trunk. That's because the trunk has no bones. It's made of more than 40,000 muscles. You have just 639 muscles in your entire body!

An elephant can easily lift a 600-pound (272.2-kilogram) log with its trunk. It can pick up a tiny, flat coin with the same ease. That's because the end of its trunk has "fingers." Asian elephants use their single finger in a grasp hold. African elephants curl their two fingers into a pinch hold. Put your thumb and pointer finger together to form a circle. That's how African elephants hold things!

Elephants depend on their trunks to feel what's nearby. They thump the ground with their trunks to make sure it's stable. They swing at, rub, and wrap their trunks on objects that cross their path. They poke and point with their trunks to communicate with their herd.

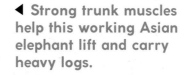

◄ Strong trunk muscles help this working Asian elephant lift and carry heavy logs.

Family Matters

Elephants live in large groups called herds. The herd is made up of adult females, called cows, and their young, called calves.

Adult cows and their calves travel together in the herd. Bulls, or male elephants, stay with the herd until they reach maturity. Then they leave their families to live separately.

The oldest cow is the **matriarch**. She leads the herd. The matriarch knows where to find the best food, how to find water during the dry season, and how to care for newborns. She warns her family of dangers and directs them to move quickly. She passes all her knowledge down to her daughters, granddaughters, sisters, and nieces.

Young cows watch the older females closely and copy their movements. Learning from one another is critical for the herd. Without older females to show what to do, cows can't learn the skills they need for survival.

▶ Sometimes herds join to comprise hundreds or even thousands of animals.

14

CHAPTER 2

Larger Than Life

African elephants weigh about 6 tons (5.4 tonnes) on average. Asian elephants average about 3.75 tons (3.4 tonnes). So it takes a lot of food to make them feel full. One adult can eat up to 200 lb. (90.7 kg) of **vegetation** daily. They often have to walk all day to find enough to eat in a given area.

All that food gets washed down with about 80 gallons (302.8 liters) of water. Although an elephant's trunk looks like a straw, the animal doesn't swallow water through it. Instead, it can use its trunk to suck up 2 gal. (7.6 l) of water at a time. Then the elephant curls its trunk to its mouth and lets go for a refreshing gulp.

During the dry season, staying **hydrated** can be a challenge. So elephants put their tusks and trunks to work. They find water by digging up dry riverbeds. They also break up the ground around trees to get water near the roots.

▶ An elephant can stretch far and high to reach the tastiest leaves.

Fast Fact
Elephant calls
can be heard
over 100 sq. mi.
(259 sq. km).

Speaking Elephant

Elephants are known for their loud trumpet blasts. But did you know that an elephant also grunts like a horse and roars like a lion? In fact, scientists have identified more than 70 different elephant calls. A short bark warns others of danger. A series of grunts attracts mates. Low rumbles get the herd to move quickly.

Many of the noises elephants make—and hear—are outside the range of human hearing. They are called **infrasonic** sounds. Elephants use their feet to detect these sounds. And we can't hear them at all. Elephants seek other herds and mates by using low-pitched calls. These rumbles travel more than 6 miles (9.7 kilometers). When the sound is received, the other elephant sends back a response.

An elephant that has been accidentally separated from its herd also **emits** a low call. It waits to hear a response, then walks toward the sound. The elephants will continue to call and respond until they are reunited.

◀ **Elephants
may trumpet to
express excitement.**

Ear Signals

An African elephant's ears measure one-sixth of its entire body. So it's no surprise elephants are super listeners! On an average day, they hear noises more than 2 mi. (1.6 km) away. In a quiet environment, they can detect sounds as far away as 6 mi. (9.7 km). They're also pros at localizing, or figuring out where a sound is coming from. An elephant will stroll toward a good sound, like a waterfall. It will move away from a dangerous noise, like the call of a **predator**.

Elephants also use their ears for more than just listening. Most people can't wiggle their ears without touching them. For elephants, it's a snap. They can move them, flap them, and fan them out. An elephant's ears are just one more way these animals talk to one another. They use their ears to signal danger or strong feelings.

Elephants flutter their ears for a friendly greeting. When an elephant shakes its ears and head rapidly, that's a sign of anger or alarm. An elephant that spreads its ears wide is doing so to appear larger. It may be presenting a bold front to another animal that appears threatening.

◄ An elephant may spread its ears and charge if it feels threatened.

Living Large

As she matures, a female elephant becomes ready to mate. She goes into **estrus** once a year for 15 to 18 weeks. During this time, her body gets ready for pregnancy. She sends out loud mating calls to bring the bulls near. She has a better chance of getting pregnant if she mates with a 40- to 50-year-old bull.

An older, experienced bull relies on his trunk to begin the mating process. He can pick up scents as far away as 12 mi. (19.3 km). When the bull detects a cow's scent, he moves toward the smell. He sniffs the ground for a trail of urine. The scent of certain chemicals tells the bull if the cow is mature enough to mate.

To be sure the cow is ready to mate, the bull may even taste her waste! The bull lifts it to a **gland** on the roof of his mouth. The gland sends signals to his brain. This tells the bull if he has found the right female to mate with.

▶ A male African elephant sniffs the air for a mate.

Protecting the Little Ones

An elephant has the longest pregnancy in the animal kingdom: 22 months. In the wild, one calf is usually born into a herd each year.

When a female is ready to give birth, the herd gathers together. The older females form a tight circle around the cow as her baby is being born. Young elephants can fall **prey** to lions and hyenas. This great gray wall keeps predators from approaching. If a predator tries to come near, members of the herd charge at it, roaring and rumbling loudly.

Minutes after the calf's birth, the herd greets the newborn with rumbles and trumpets. The older cows encourage and nudge the calf to stand up. When the baby takes its wobbly first steps, it stays close to its mom. Within an hour, the calf is ready to **nurse**.

While the mom feeds her calf, the herd gets to work covering up any signs of the birth. They use their trunks to spray dirt over damp areas and scatter a layer of grass on the ground. This keeps predators from sniffing out the helpless calf.

▶ A newborn calf weighs 200 lb. (90.7 kg) and can stand within minutes.

Fast Fact
Calves are about
3 ft. (.9 m) tall
at birth.

Baby Steps

The herd gives the mom and baby a few days to **bond**. When they're ready to roam, the calf walks under its mother. The herd slows its pace so the baby can keep up. As the mom pauses to eat, her calf nurses.

Feeding a calf is very demanding. A baby elephant drinks 10 pints (4.7 liters) of milk each day! A human newborn drinks less than 1 pt. (0.5 l) of its mother's milk daily. The calf nurses every few minutes, or whenever its mom stops walking. To make sure the new mom eats and rests enough, other members of the herd take turns babysitting the newborn.

◀ Baby elephants are surrounded by attentive relatives at all times.

29

Ready to Roam

It takes a calf several weeks to figure out its trunk. At first, it swings it around clumsily. Eventually, it gets the hang of it. By four months old, the calf can grab leaves and branches to eat. The calf will nurse for two more years, but **foraging** becomes a bigger part of its day.

A female calf stays close to her mom for the first few years of her life. She won't wander away—unlike male calves that wander up to nearby bulls. They notice how the bulls behave. They learn how to display **dominance** and how to back off from older bulls. These informal lessons get the young bull ready to leave its herd. If a male hasn't ditched his herd by age 12, his female family will push him out!

Bulls wander off alone or join other young bulls in a bachelor herd. Males come and go in this herd as they search for a mate. If a bull meets his family herd again during his travels, the cows celebrate. They trumpet loudly. They stroke him with their trunks. Then they send him back on his way.

▶ Males often spend time alone. Those with large tusks are called tuskers.

CHAPTER 4

Then and Now

Elephant ancestry dates back over 55 million years. Scientists believe there were more than 300 species of Proboscidea. Today, elephants are the only surviving members of the order. *Moeritherium*, the first **ancestor** we know about, lived on land and in water in northern Africa. It didn't have a long trunk, and it was much smaller than today's elephants. It looked like a cross between a hippopotamus and a tapir.

As time went on, elephants **adapted** to their environment. For example, the woolly mammoth, which lived during the last Ice Age, grew thick, long hair.

Primelephas, which is considered the latest common ancestor of both African and Asian elephants, lived about 4 million years ago. The major difference between *Primelephas* and today's elephants is its tusks. It had two long upper tusks and two short lower tusks. Over time, the lower tusks disappeared completely from the species.

▶ The woolly mammoth's massive tusks were 15 ft. (4.6 m) long.

Humans and Elephants

Humans and elephants have worked together for more than 6,000 years. Ancient armies rode elephants into battle. People used them as transportation to get through difficult terrain.

Even today, more than 10,000 **captive** elephants work in Asia. Elephants help pull machinery that's used to clear fields. Then they haul away heavy tree trunks. One working elephant can carry up to 4 tons (3.6 tonnes) per day. That's about two times as heavy as a car!

Elephants are considered **sacred** animals in many parts of Asia. For this reason, temples and prominent people may own and keep elephants. These elephants are trained to participate in religious parades and festivals. Their faces are painted with bright paints. Their bodies are draped in colorful cloths.

For nearly 150 years, Ringling Bros. and Barnum & Bailey Circus had the largest Asian elephant herd in its performances. In 2016, the circus retired its herd. The elephants, mostly female, now live full-time at Ringling's Center for Elephant Conservation in Florida.

◄ Asian elephants participate in festivals and parades in India.

CHAPTER 5

A Future at Risk

At the start of the 1900s, there were several million African elephants and more than 100,000 Asian elephants in the wild. Today, those numbers have dropped sharply. Asian elephants number just 40,000. Their African cousins number less than 600,000.

Conservation scientists first listed Asian elephants as endangered in 1986. In 2012, the Sumatran elephant was changed to critically endangered. This subspecies lost half its population in just one generation.

African elephants are listed as vulnerable. Scientists believe their numbers are rising slowly each year. In some areas of Africa, the number of animals has declined. In other parts, their population has risen. Over time, this balances out the African elephant population.

Threats to these magnificent beasts include loss of habitat and poaching.

▶ Elephants in India face severe deforestation.

Working for Change

Over the years, people have moved into areas where elephants traditionally lived. They clear forests and grasslands to build homes and plant farms. As elephants' habitat shrinks, food becomes harder to find. Elephants sometimes travel into villages. They destroy crops and trample farms. The elephants are often killed.

The Elephant Flying Squad in Sumatra is trying to help. This group of trained elephants and their mahouts scare wandering elephants back into the wild before they can do any damage or get hurt.

Environmentalists also work with farmers to protect their crops. Elephants don't like the smell of lemon, so farmers plant lemon trees around their farms. Others plant cactus or thorny plants to keep the elephants away.

Believe it or not, bees are also helping to keep elephants safe. Elephants don't like small critters, especially insects. So farmers outline their land with honeybee hives. The hives keep elephants away from crops while also providing income from honey for farmers.

◀ Elephants are great swimmers. The animal's trunk acts as a snorkel.

No More Ivory Trade

Buying and selling ivory has been illegal around the world since 1989. Still, about 27,000 elephants are killed each year for their tusks. And ivory continues to be sold illegally on the black market, where it is used for trinkets and jewelry.

To steal ivory tusks, poachers often slaughter entire herds, leaving just the baby elephants behind. Without the help of their herds, many orphaned calves soon die, too. The Elephant Orphanage Project in Africa set out to change that. It rescues young elephants who have survived poaching attacks. The babies are cared for at a nursery near Kafue National Park in Zambia. About 1,000 wild elephants live at the park. As the orphans get stronger, they roam into the park. Over time, they join the wild elephants. Special collars track them to see how they adapt to life in the wild.

Thanks to efforts around the world, Asian and African elephants now have a better chance for survival. There may be hope for these gentle giants after all.

▶ Illegal ivory is often burned to discourage poachers.

Elephant Family Tree

Elephants are mammals. Mammals are warm-blooded animals that have hair or fur and usually give birth to live babies; female mammals produce milk to feed their young. Mammals comprise more than 5,000 species. They all share a common ancestor that lived 100 million years ago. This diagram shows how elephants are related to some other mammals. The closer together two animals are on the tree, the more similar they are.

Aardvarks
pig-sized mammals with big snouts for smelling insects

Elephant Shrews
small, insect-eating mammals with long tails and snouts

Armadillos
insect-eating mammals with long snouts and bony armor

Sloths
furry, tree-dwelling mammals with long limbs and curved claws

Ancestor of all Mammals

Note: Animal photos are not to scale.

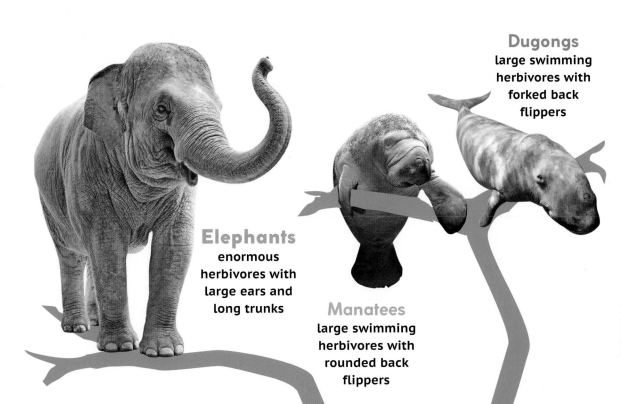

Dugongs
large swimming
herbivores with
forked back
flippers

Elephants
enormous
herbivores with
large ears and
long trunks

Manatees
large swimming
herbivores with
rounded back
flippers

Hydraxes
furry, rabbit-sized
herbivores with
short tails

Words to Know

A .... **adapted** *(ad-ap-TED)* changed or improved to better fit into one's environment

ancestor *(ANN-ses-tur)* a family member who lived long ago

B .... **bond** *(BAHND)* to form a close connection with or strong feeling for someone

C .... **captive** *(KAP-tiv)* living in the care of people

D .... **dominance** *(DAH-muh-nents)* position of power

E .... **emits** *(i-MITS)* produces or sends out something, such as heat, light, signals, or sound

endangered *(en-DAYN-juhrd)* a plant or animal that is in danger of becoming extinct, usually because of human activity

estrus *(ESS-trus)* a periodic state during which the female of most mammals is willing to mate with the male and is capable of becoming pregnant

extinct *(ik-STINGKT)* no longer found alive

F .... **foraging** *(FOR-ij-ing)* going in search of food

G .... **gestures** *(JES-churz)* actions that show feelings

gland *(GLAND)* an organ in the body that produces or releases natural chemicals

H .... **habitat** *(HAB-i-tat)* the place where an animal or plant is usually found

hydrated *(HYE-dray-ted)* supplied with enough fluid or moisture

I .... **incisor** *(in-SYE-zur)* a kind of tooth in the front of the mouth that is used for cutting

infrasonic *(in-fruh-SAH-nik)* a sound too low for the human ear to hear

M.......... **mammals** *(MAM-uhlz)* warm-blooded animals that have hair or fur and usually give birth to live babies; female mammals produce milk to feed their young

matriarch *(MAY-tree-ark)* a female who rules a family, group, or state

N .... **nurse** *(NURS)* drink milk from a breast

P .... **poachers** *(POHCH-uhrz)* people who hunt or fish illegally on someone else's property

predator *(PRED-uh-tuhr)* an animal that lives by hunting other animals for food

prey *(PRAY)* an animal that is hunted by another animal for food

S .... **sacred** *(SAY-krid)* holy, or having to do with religion

savanna *(suh-VAN-uh)* a flat, grassy plain with few or no trees

species *(SPEE-sheez)* one of the groups into which animals and plants are divided; members of the same species can mate and have offspring

synchronized *(SING-kruh-nized)* happening at the same time

T .... **tsunami** *(tsu-NAH-mee)* a very large, destructive wave caused by an underwater earthquake or volcano

V .... **vegetation** *(vej-i-TAY-shuhn)* plant life or the plants that cover an area

vulnerable *(VUHL-nur-uh-buhl)* a species that is facing threats and is likely to become endangered

Find Out More

BOOKS

- Anthony, Lawrence. *The Elephant Whisperer: My Life with the Herd in the African Wild*. New York: St. Martin's Griffin, 2009.
- Downer, Ann. *Elephant Talk: The Surprising Science of Elephant Communication*. Minneapolis, MN: Twenty-First Century Books, 2011.
- Marsh, Laura. *Great Migrations: Elephants*. Washington, D.C.: National Geographic Society, 2010.

WEB PAGES

- www.npr.org/2015/08/20/432616506/to-decode-elephant-conversation-you-must-feel-the-jungle-rumble

  Learn more about elephant communication from NPR's *Science Friday*.
- animals.sandiegozoo.org/animals/elephant

  This San Diego Zoo site offers sound samples and a link to a Webcam.
- www.pbs.org/wnet/nature/elephants-africa-life-elephant/11382

  The PBS *Nature* documentary, "The Elephants of Africa," and its companion Web site discuss the life cycle of elephants, as well as the dangers they face.

Facts for Now

Visit this Scholastic Web site for more information on elephants:
www.factsfornow.scholastic.com Enter the keyword Elephants

Index

Index *(continued)*

About the Author

Anna Prokos has written countless stories about animals and the environment. She especially admires elephants and their female herds—that's because her clan is all male! Anna lives with her husband and four amazing boys in North Carolina.